FROM PEN TO PUBLISHED

A BLUEPRINT FOR SUCCESS

BUILD YOUR BOOK
BRICK BY BRICK

BRANDON WILLIAMS
AND MICHELLE HILL

ISBN: 978-1-7346467-1-9

Publishing date: 7/20/2020
Cover Design by MASgraphicarts.com

DEDICATION

To all of you who are brave enough to step out of your comfort zone and get your book done, we dedicate this book to you.

You are indeed a rare breed and now you're a giant step ahead of all the rest who will only ever think and talk about writing and publishing a book yet do nothing to get it done.

You are the bold one!

The courageous one!

The winning one!

Here's to YOU!

TABLE OF CONTENTS

INTRODUCTION

*"Let us answer a book of ink with
a book of flesh and blood."*

— Ralph Waldo Emerson

We wrote this book to help you build your words into a published book, brick by brick. We wrote this book for YOU! You have a story to tell and we want to help you get that story out of your head and heart and onto the page.

If you're a speaker, having a book to sell after your speaking events will bolster your credibility as an expert and provide attendees a way to 'take you home' with them. If you're a businessman, you need a book to tell people what you have learned along the way about leadership, success, and personal freedom.

If you're an entrepreneur and want to leverage the vast knowledge and expertise you've amassed, a book is a sure bet to establish yourself as an expert. By using the analogy of building a house, we're going to show you how to build a book, what goes into the infrastructure, and how to put the finishing touches on your masterpiece.

In chapter one we'll discuss the importance of selecting a location for your book; this means determining your target market, your ideal reader; who you would like to impact with your book. We'll design your writing house by creating a floorplan through the mind-mapping process and show how it unleashes your creative power.

In chapter two we move onto finding an accountability partner to keep you on track. You'll find out how to choose the right person who will motivate you and help you conquer any obstacles that get in your way.

Chapter three is an important chapter because that's where you'll build an outline which is like laying the footings for a house. First, we'll examine how the integrity of the house depends on how strong the footings are, and the second section will show you how to build upon a solid foundation of details. This is where we'll show you exactly how to develop a structurally sound outline.

In chapter four we put up the drywall of your book by marking the locations of your daily writing time studs, cutting out specific blocks of time, and attaching yourself to your schedule with concentrated effort.

Chapter five takes you further by showing you how to create quality audio recordings which is like installing doors and windows in your writing house. First, we'll show you how to air out and let go of your stale stories and let in fresh, energetic stories that your readers will relate to. You'll learn how to organize your recordings to make it easier to decipher when you get them transcribed into Word documents. Then we'll tell you exactly how to get your recordings into said documents, which is kind of like putting a roof on your writing house. A high-quality shingle roof protects you from outside elements. Seeing your words hung like shingles on the paper protects you from a weak storyline and exposes leaks, cracks, moss, and rust in your manuscript.

In chapter six you'll discover how to wire your manuscript by conducting thorough research to uncover facts and statistics that support your book's main theme, correctly sourcing the facts you do find, and putting the spark into your manuscript by unearthing stories within the stories. There are always details and nuances between the lines!

Chapter seven is the plumbing chapter. Proper plumbing in a house ensures long-term durability and stability. We'll tell you about the three main pipes you must include in your writing house: 1) your personality pipe, 2) your personal style and flair pipe, and 3) your unique mannerisms and sensory details pipe. Using this piping system ensures a strong, smooth-flowing manuscript.

Chapter eight is all about vulnerability. Once you've completed the first draft of your book, it's time to show it to a couple of trusted...very trusted...friends and colleagues for feedback. This phase of critiquing and constructive criticism is the most difficult part of the journey.

It's like painting your favorite room of the house—choosing and blending colors and textures make the walls stand out even better, yet everyone has their opinion of what looks the best. We'll talk about how to go about choosing the right reviewers to make your book even better.

If chapter eight was painful, chapter nine is no better, for this is where we begin the editing process. Editing is like furnishing a home; you must determine what goes where, what stays, what goes, and what needs replacing. It can be painful because whatever does not move your manuscript forward must be moved out of the way, and some of your favorite manuscript "furniture" might include a good sectional that is too big for the room. In chapter ten we add accent pieces to your completed writing house.

Your manuscript is done and adding the right accents will make it a real home. We'll discuss essential accents like securing a great book formatter, cover designer, promo site designer, and we'll give you some tips on how to find the right publisher. In this chapter we also cover tipping ladders: what pitfalls and dangers to watch out for when building a house/book. Eg: writing and editing at the same time, procrastinating, expecting perfection, securing "cheap" vendors, enlisting friends/family to edit your book.

Chapter eleven provides a writing rescue when the process seems too daunting, or you just don't have the time or writing ability to tackle a book project on your own. Writing your own book or entrusting the process to a professional who can get it done seamlessly is similar to decorating your home on your own without proper color, texture and neuro-architecture knowledge and hiring a professional decorator who knows exactly what to do to beautify your home.

Chapter twelve, "Hanging Artwork," provides helpful mental and visual motivation tips to get you through the entire process of getting your book published.

When you're done reading this book, you'll have all the tools necessary to build your "book house." You'll have a finished manuscript, ready for publishing. We'll also provide a solution in case this all seems too overwhelming. We've unlocked all the doors for you to step through the threshold into the new world of being a published author.

Now let's start building your writing house!

PART I
THE FOUNDATION

1

YOUR BOOK'S FLOOR PLAN
DESIGNING A STRATEGY THAT WORKS

*"Every secret of a writer's soul, every experience
of his life, every quality of his mind, is written
large in his works."*

— Virginia Woolf

This chapter is all about building your book's foundation. I'm a proponent of creating an outline in the way that works best with your brain whether it be mind-mapping, a traditional outline, which we'll cover later in this eBook, good old-fashioned pen and paper, or through PowerPoint.

Mind-mapping is a free flow process of ideas without judgement or opinion. You're simply brainstorming all the ideas, great and small, for your book. No idea is stupid. No idea is too small. No idea is too big. After all, since your ideas flow out of you, we're going to take all your wonderful ideas and design a strategy, a floorplan. Use your mindmap to also answer the "why" of writing your book and the audiences you want to reach.

A homebuilder doesn't just start slapping a house up haphazardly without a plan; if he did, it would end up looking like a monstrosity when it is finished. No, the homebuilder designs a floorplan so he and his workers know where the walls, the doors, the windows, and the rooms are supposed to go. Before he starts to build, he prepares the ground so the house doesn't lean to one side. He must start with a level playing field, so to speak.

Before we start the mind-mapping process, let's move some dirt around so we begin our building on level ground. Let's quickly excavate your excuses—move them out of the way—so you can allow your ideas to move easily from your heart onto the paper. You probably have a few rocky excuses hanging around that have prevented you from getting your book done, or even started.

These excuses might sound something like:

"I just have too much going on right now to think about writing a book."

"I'm not really that great of a writer."

"My family needs me so I can't really devote any time to writing."

"Nobody would want to read what I have to say anyway."

Do you have a different excuse that has prevented you from writing the book you know would transform people's lives? Let's hear it.

Okay? Got 'em all out?

Good, your excuses are out on the table. Face them, feel them, and then put them in the dumpster and let's start working.

Mind-mapping

This is how you start: Using a free mindmap program like mindup.com (a quick Google search will reveal other free mind-mapping software) and create at least a hundred thoughts about your book idea.

Traditional Outline

We'll cover the traditional outline in Chapter 3.

PowerPoint

If you're a highly visual person you may want to consider creating a PowerPoint presentation, each slide representing the chapters of your book, your ideas, possible titles/sub-titles, and any references you want to utilize. Since this is for your eyes only, no need to create a fancy presentation.

• Good Old-fashioned Pen & Paper

This is for all the old-school people out there! You like the feel of paper and a pencil/pen in your hand. You can also use a sharpie and poster board. Start with a central theme in the middle by drawing a circle and writing your book title or the main topic you want to focus on and start adding ideas that build on that central theme. You can break your thoughts up into chapter bubbles and then add sub-ideas under each chapter. The idea is to allow your mind free association to just create. This is not the time to judge your ideas. If you are writing your autobiography, include ideas that have to do with your major life events, stories, and relationships. This process works whether you have a super organized mind or a mind that works in fragmented bits.

Start with your childhood and move forward. Once you connect the dots of all your life stories, you will have a loose blueprint upon which to build your manuscript. If you're writing an informational or motivational-type book you will still want to include personal stories but you will list the major topics you want to include in your book.

• Table of Contents

If the outline task makes you want to vomit, instead, create a working Table of Contents. You can divide your manuscript into major sections like Part I, II, etc. or you can give it four quarters like in a football or basketball game.

• Your Design Strategy

This section is all about details. Stay with us here. Even if you're not a detailed person, in order to build a house, there are certain critical details that need to be discussed: What kind of piping will you use? What type of plumbing? How many cupboards in the kitchen? And, especially, how many bathrooms will there be and where will they go? The details for your book include figuring out the following:

- Who is your target audience? Your answer should not be everyone. That's too broad. You must have a specific reader in mind. That's not to say your book can't have mass market appeal but your focus should stay on a specific group of people. Are your target readers business start-ups? Successful entrepreneurs who want to move to the next level? Young adults who need guidance and motivation? Kids? Those who have gone through a specific life storm? This eBook is targeted toward success-oriented adults who want to write and publish a book. Simple and straightforward.

- What categories will your book be listed in on the major online booksellers? (Self-help, motivation, autobiographical, business principles, humor, etc.)

- What tone and style do you want your book to portray? (serious, humorous, combination of both, business-like, casual).

These are just a few things to consider as you lay the foundation for your book. Now, we move onto the next phase of your journey – accountability.

2

KEEPIN' IT 100
ACCOUNTABILITY COUNTS

*"If you hang out with chickens, you're going to cluck
and if you hang out with eagles, you're going to soar."*

— **Virginia Woolf**

Before any builder starts a project, he obtains construction insurance. In fact, he cannot start to build anything unless he has it. Having good builder liability insurance coverage can protect against injuries, accidents or property damage suffered on the job. The same goes for building your book, except your construction insurance consists of obtaining an accountability partner. Your accountability partner will keep you focused on your book writing journey AND the destination…finishing.

An accountability partner will call you once a week to ask you a series of questions that might range from, "How many pages did you get done?" "What challenges did you encounter?" And, "What is your goal for next week?"

It's not a good idea to enlist a family member or friend as your accountability partner because there is too much familiarity. You need a professional book writing coach to guide you to completion of your book.

In the Bonus Chapter, we'll provide tips on how to stay motivated while you're writing but for now, just know that you must become comfortable with receiving constructive criticism. An accountability coach will only serve to make your book better and stronger, and as a result, he or she will tell you when your manuscript falls short or areas where it needs more development. Don't be one of those prima donna writers where you believe YOUR words are the only ones that count. Remain open to positive critique and feedback – and by positive we don't mean you're going to hear all affirming comments, praising your superb writing talent in awe and wonder. By positive feedback we mean feedback that pokes holes in your manuscript so you can fill them with more substance; the substance that will keep your readers engaged and turning every page in anticipation. Now we move to laying the footings for your manuscript. However you started out—mind-mapping, pen and paper, PowerPoint—a solid outline really IS your friend and we're going to discover why in Chapter 3!

3

GET YOUR BOOK FOOTINGS
LAID IN THE GOOD SOIL
THE POWER OF AN OUTLINE

"I would advise anyone who aspires to a writing career that before developing his talent he would be wise to develop a thick hide."

— Harper Lee, American novelist widely known for To Kill a Mockingbird, published in 1960

Without strong footings, a house will not stand erect. Footings for a house are as your feet and legs are to your body. Footings anchor your home to the ground and provide support for its foundation, which in turn carries the weight of your house.

What does all that have to do with your book? The strength of your outline acts as the footings for your manuscript. The stronger the outline, the stronger your book will be. Weak footings can compromise the strength of a house just like a weak, sparse outline will compromise the strength of your book.

Footings need to be placed in good soil, and your good soil represents building an organized outline with a main book theme that will make sense to you tomorrow AND next week.

Your mind-mapping exercise should have helped you in organizing your thoughts and ideas. If you create a vague, disconnected outline, you will go back to it and wonder what the heck you were thinking. If your content baffles you, it will baffle your readers. Start by choosing your main book topic (refer to your mind-mapping session) and write one sentence that describes the overall theme of your book. Using Roman Numerals for the headings, write a few words for each of your chapter topics.

Now that you've laid the footings, let's tackle the foundation of your writing house in Part II.

• How to Add Concrete Details to Your Outline

Pouring a solid foundation for a house provides strength and design flexibility as well as fire resistance. What that means for your book is that a detailed outline will provide a strong structure for your main theme and resistance against outside influences who will always have an opinion about your book. Even though, unlike a mindmap, an outline is structured, it still provides design flexibility to change topics or order if something is just not working in the manuscript.

Once you complete the Roman Numerals for each chapter topic, which I suggest doing first, add the following details: 1) Use capital letters for your sub-topics, and 2) Add two points for each point under the sub-topic.

• Example of Outline Structure:

Main Topic (thesis statement about what book is about)

I. Chapter #1 title

    A. Sub-topic #1

        1. sub-point #1

        2. sub-point #2

II. Chapter #2

and so on…

Now that you have strong footings and a solid foundation, it's time to create a consistent writing schedule. Let's jump in!

PART II

THE STRUCTURE

4

JUST SAY IT
WHAT TO DO IF WRITING ISN'T YOUR THING

"The more you sweat in practice, the less you bleed in battle."

— **Author Unknown**

When you install doors and windows into your new home's structure, you create an opportunity for light to enter and illuminate each room. An ample supply of windows allows fresh air to come in, and each door provides a gateway to enter or exit a room. What your ultimate goal should be is to open the doors and windows of your manuscript by letting in fresh, energetic stories, and using proper comparisons, and time/order sequences that are relatable to readers.

But what if there were no windows and doors in your house? Wouldn't it feel more like a prison than a house? That's what it can feel like if you just don't possess the writing skill to produce a full-length manuscript…even a short one.

But, if writing just isn't your thing, what do you do?

You just say it!

Some people are simply better at talking out their ideas than writing them down or typing them. You might be one of those people! At this point, you may be thinking, "Yowzers, I will never get my book done because I just don't feel confident in my writing ability. Heck, I have trouble writing out a shopping list."

It's okay. Here's how to speak your manuscript.

- You can either invest $60 - $100 for a high-quality digital recording device or you can use a free app on your phone like Cogi or Hi-Q but make absolutely sure whatever app you use can be downloaded as an MP3 digital recording that you can either save to Dropbox or share via email. Practice with it because what you don't want to happen is for all your hard work to fly out the window because it wasn't recorded, or worse yet, to push the wrong button by accident and erase an entire recording.

- To keep audios organized, speak chapter and section titles BEFORE you start speaking your content.

- Keep your speaking pace steady and include as many sensory details as possible. Eg: How you felt emotionally, what you saw, what you heard, how a particular room smelled, or how a certain food item tasted during your experience. Did items around you feel new, worn, or smooth/rough to the touch? You can use any and all of your senses depending on the situation you're describing.

- Tell your stories like you're talking to a friend sitting across from you. Stiff, format, polite storytelling will be boring to your readers. If it helps, visualize a specific friend. Tell your stories as you would to your best friend.

*"Push yourself again and again. Don't give an inch
until the final buzzer sounds."*

— Larry Bird

Getting Your Voice Down on Paper

This section covers putting the roof on your audio recordings by getting them transcribed into Word documents. Just like a roof inspection reveals leaks, cracks, moss, and rust, seeing your words in written form will also expose leaks in your storyline, cracks in the structure of your content, the moss of stale, boring stories, and the rust of faulty research or information.

Okay, so once you've recorded all your chapters, you'll want to get them transcribed into Word documents so you have the basic structure for your book. You'll do this by enlisting the services of a great, not good, great, transcriber. Our recommendation is to stay away from services offered from foreign countries. For this portion of your book journey, it's best to stay with native-US, English-as-a-first-language professionals.

Once you receive the written document, organize it into logical chapters and sections. It won't all make sense at this point but at least you'll have a structure from which to work. Then add the extra pages that every book must have; these pages will be placeholders for the actual information. In the first pages, include: title page, title/sub-title page, ISBN publishing page, dedication page, if any, and Table of Content page. You may also have a preface and a Foreword (not always needed). If you haven't included the Introduction in your recordings, add a placeholder page for it as it's often the last thing you will write).

For the back of the book, add placeholder pages for your conclusion, about the author, acknowledgements, references, and how to order/contact.

5

IF WRITING *IS* YOUR THING
HOW TO SCREW TIME INTO YOUR
SCHEDULE FOR WRITING

"If you are determined enough and willing to pay the price, you can get it done."

— Mike Ditka, former American football player, coach, and television commentator

Putting up the drywall for your manuscript means marking the locations of the daily time studs, cutting out specific blocks of time, and attaching yourself to that block of time in a concentrated effort.

Here are some tips on how to set a writing schedule:

13. **Create an editorial calendar.** You can either use a large desk calendar, an erasable wall calendar, or on online calendar that syncs with your phone.

14. **Block specific time periods each day when you're most productive.** What time zone is your personal body clock on? Do you work best at 5:00 a.m. Or are you a night owl who will write pages and pages at midnight or 1:00 a.m.? Create a writing schedule that

works for you! Whatever your magic time zone formula is, use it to your advantage.

15.   Createawritingspacethatispleasantandinviting. If you don't, you won't write. A clean, organized space promotes creativity and makes you more efficient. Light a couple of candles if that helps inspire you. Turn on some relaxing background music but not too loud or it will be a distraction. Keep a bottle of water on your desk so you don't have to interrupt your work flow.

16.   Buildin20minutesadaytoreadbooksyoulike. By reading a few pages a day and studying different authors' writing styles will make you a better writer.

17.   Don'tmisstwodaysinarownomatterwhat! You wouldn't dream of missing two days without brushing your teeth or taking a shower or combing your hair... would you? Schedule your writing into your daily schedule and stick to it like your life depends on it.

Keep up your writing schedule until you have a solid rough draft to work with. Don't worry or obsess about your page count. Our philosophy is - Tell your story, then stop. If you get hung up on having 200 pages and you've told your story and included all the details in 150 pages, then everything beyond that is just fluff. You want to keep your readers engaged and turning pages until the end. Also, in today's day and age, most people do not have the time or the patience to read a 300-page monster of a book. Take a look at the following timeless classics and their page count.

Ernest Hemingway's The Old Man and the Sea, is 128 pages.

George Clason's The Richest Man in Babylon, is 144 pages.

Russell Conwell's Acres of Diamonds, is 92 pages.

Charles Dickens' A Christmas Carol, is 78 pages.

Wallace D. Wattles' The Science of Getting Rich is 61 pages.

See what I mean?

If you've screwed time into your daily schedule for writing, you should have completed the first draft of your manuscript! Excited? You should be! This is a major accomplishment that most people will never realize.

So, now what? Research is the name of the game and it's YOUR job to get it done prudently and wisely. Let's dig in.

6

ADD SPARK TO YOUR WRITING
WITH CAREFUL RESEARCH

"Let the world burn through you. Throw the prism light, white hot, on paper."

— **Ray Bradbury**

Wiring a house involves adding switches, lights, and receptacles and it all has to be done with the proper codes and permits. In addition, an electrician will install low-voltage lights, airtight recessed lights, and LED lights as well as security lights around the house. Wiring a house for efficiency involves precision and placement.

The best way to "wire" your manuscript is with precisely-placed supporting facts, studies, and short quotes from similar topic books.

When you want to source facts in your manuscript, you can either use footnotes or include a resource section in the back of your book; sometimes both. And this is where you can run into some high-voltage situations. The biggest issue to consider is:

Don't plagiarize unless you really enjoy being in court!

The basics: (note: Brandon Williams and Michelle Hill are not legal advisors and the following does not constitute legal counsel. When using others' content, please consult the advice of a copyright attorney.)

1. Anything written before 1923 is public domain and can be used without copyright permission.

2. What constitutes having to gain written permission depends on whom you ask. Some people say 300 words. Some say one line. Some say 10% of the word count. It's generally okay to quote a line from another author but any more than that and you open yourself up to fair use violation even though there are no "official" legal "rules" that dictate where and when violations occur.

3. Song lyrics cannot be used...ever...unless of course they're YOUR song lyrics. You'll still see partial song lyrics in books but technically they're not supposed to be there and the author and publisher could get sued if caught.

Here are three fabulous websites that contain pertinent information on fair use guidelines:

1. https://janefriedman.com/permissions/

2. https://janefriedman.com/the-fair-use-doctrine/

3. https://www.thebookdesigner.com/2010/02/what-every-writer-ought-to-know-about-fair-use-and-copyright/

An absolutely awesome source for you to gather expert opinions and quotes for your book is profnet.com. You can sign up for FREE as an expert or as a journalist. Enter your parameters and they will send you what you're looking for. And it's all fair use so there's no need to spend any time asking/begging for permissions.

Another way to add a jolt to your manuscript is to do some sleuthing by researching your competition just for comparison sake. Go to your favorite online bookseller or even your local library and find out how authors who have written similar books have presented their material. Study different writing styles and how your competition challenges their readers. Of course, you'll need to keep true to your own writing style but you can pick up a ton of pointers by reading books that are in the same genre as yours.

Now, we turn our attention to the small "plumbing adjustments" in your manuscript—the little details that make a big difference.

7

THE JOY OF PLUMBING WORDS INTO A SMOOTH-FLOWING MANUSCRIPT

"Don't try to figure out what other people want to hear from you; figure out what you have to say. It's the one and only thing you have to offer."

— Barbara Kingsolver

The plumbing in a house pieces everything together and makes the water flow smoothly into your faucets. Anything goes wrong and you have a major problem on your hands. The plumbing for your manuscript is like fitting pipes together. Your personality. Your style and flair. Your mannerisms. They all fit together to make your manuscript YOURS! Let's look at adding a few of the pipes that will make your writing uniquely yours.

Pipe #1 – Add Your Personality. Add your distinctive personality to every line. Although you may admire another person's writing, don't try to copy it. You were born with a specialized set of personality traits, both good and bad, and you want that to shine through when you write and/or speak your chapters.

Pipe #2 – Add Your Personal Style and Flair. What is your style? Is it laid-back? Aggressive? Smooth and charming?

Happy-go-lucky? Maybe a combination of a couple? There's a jazz club/restaurant in Durham, North Carolina called Beyu Caffe. The mantra is, "Just come and be you." Well, that's exactly what you need to do with your manuscript. Just be you! You possess flair…you know you do. Use your flair to wow your readers.

Dictionary.com   (http://www.dictionary.com/browse/flair) describes flair as:

1. a natural talent, aptitude, or ability; bent; knack: a flair for rhyming.

2. smartness of style, manner, etc.:
   Their window display has absolutely no flair at all.
   Synonyms: chic; dash; panache; verve; oomph; pizazz.

3. keen, intuitive perception or discernment:
   We want a casting director with a real flair for finding dramatic talent.

Pipe #3 – Add your mannerisms. Do this by using sensory details; what you saw, touched, heard, felt, and smelled. We already covered this in a previous chapter but it will serve you well if we repeat it. We've all heard it said that ten people can witness the same situation and you'll get ten different perspectives on what happened. No one can express your mannerisms quite like you so take advantage of your gift and infuse your book with the best parts of you.

Now that you've added your personality and flair, you get to step into the really fun part of writing a book. Keep scrolling to find out the next spooky step that will make the hairs on your neck stand on end.

8

PAINT ME BETTER
THE BENEFITS OF CONSTRUCTIVE
CRITICISM AND HONEST FEEDBACK

"All the words I use in my stories can be found in the dictionary – it's just a matter of arranging them into the right sentences."

— Somerset Maugham

Admit it – it's way more fun to paint your favorite room in the house rather than the exterior. And when you're painting or applying texture to the walls of your favorite room, everybody has an opinion about the outcome, right? Some might say, "Oh, too much texture." Others may chime in with, "Why did you use that color paint?" The same thing goes when you ask people to read and provide constructive criticism on what you had to say and the way you said it.

Brace yourself. Gird your loins. Be prepared.

Gathering feedback from book reviewers requires you to have tough skin and an open mind. The really scary thing about writing a book is that people will read it so choose your reviewers wisely and carefully! You don't want people who are jealous of the fact that you have a book and they don't so they proceed to rip yours to shreds. You must choose balanced, emotionally-healthy reviewers who have YOUR best interest at heart and only want to make your book better. Choose people whom you will ultimately thank for their input.

The rules of engagement for constructive criticism:

Rule #1: Don't allow anyone to prematurely see your manuscript. Work on it first, polish it second, and then work on it some more. If you allow best friends or family to peek at your manuscript before it's ready, we guarantee you'll become confused at all the "helpful" insights. You might even be tempted to scrap the whole thing and start over. Don't! Remember the color and your favorite room? Yeah, it's like that.

Rule #2: When submitting to reviewers, clearly state the following reason for your request:

a. You're gathering written testimonials for the front pages of the book

b. You want them to show you small ways to make your book better, not a complete overhaul of ideas.

Rule #3: Choose your reviewers carefully. What you're seeking here is constructive feedback on areas of your manuscript that lack luster, gaps in your stories, logical sequence of material, expansion of certain ideas, etc. When you present your manuscript to reviewers, use the watermark feature of Word to say UNEDITED VERSION. You're not looking for reviewers to point out grammar, punctuation, and spelling – your copy-editor/proofreader will do that.

Rule #4: Provide your reviewers a deadline for returning their comments. If you don't, you'll never get the feedback you want and need. Everyone is so terribly busy these days, so provide enough time for reviewers to make their comments without too much pressure, but not enough time where your book is going to get buried in a pile of email.

Rule #5: Remember, you don't have to incorporate every comment or suggestion. Read each comment or suggestion with an open mind. Ask yourself, "Will this revision make my book better?" It's your book and you get to choose what goes in and what stays out. Try your best to keep your emotions out of it because that will just muddle your thinking – keep a subjective mind about the process.

Now that your favorite room is painted and touched up with constructive feedback, you can advance to the next phase of your book – the really painful part. You're going to perform surgery on your manuscript and it's going to hurt.

PART III
THE FINISHING TOUCHES

9

OUCH, THAT HURT!
EDITING CAN BE PAINFUL

*"Writing is easy. All you have to do is cross out the
wrong words."*

— **Mark Twain**

When moving large pieces of furniture around, or carrying heavy pieces upstairs or downstairs, you're bound to get sore muscles no matter how great a shape you are. Then, you're faced with the arduous task of moving the furniture around the room until they're placed just how you (or your wife) want them. Often in a big move, you might take some extra worn-out furniture to a thrift store so you can buy fresh, new pieces for your house.

During the editing phase of your book, you're going to move the word "furniture" around – a lot! You're going to eliminate words and phrases that don't fit within your book structure and you're going to add the pieces from your reviewers that you feel fit into the general theme of your book.

After this major overhaul, you'll feel exhausted. Your brain will hurt. Your thinking muscles will need some T L C. The process will hurt because some of your precious words will need to be cut because they don't fit with the other word "furniture."

Here are a few of our best tips for the editing process:

> Mark places for smooth word and paragraph transitions.

> Measure common words for effectiveness and replace with more dynamic word choices.

> Repair rips and tears with punctuation, spelling, and grammar.

> Use tools like Copyscape (plagiarism checker) and Grammarly (grammar, spelling, punctuation, passive sentence, & sentence structure checker—both minimal cost although not a replacement for a professional editor). One thing to watch out for in Grammarly is that it can scrub your manuscript to be too sterile. Today's style of reading and writing is not always "in tune" with the old, stuffy, formal ways.

> Use the Find field in your Word document and search your manuscript for "tion" words and try to remove them. You see, "tion" words like observation began their lives as verbs but have morphed into nouns that have birthed boring words like "is" or "made." Eg: He made an observation. She worked on the translation. Turn the "tion" words back into their original form. Eg: He observed the issue. She translated the document.

> Use the Find field and search for all the "ment" words. Eg: Development > develop; Management > manage; engagement > engage.

> Use the Find field to search for "ize" words. Eg: Icky: Are you maximizing your marketing opportunities?

Better: Are you making the most from your marketing opportunities?

> Move jargon out of your writing room! Write in plain English – your readers will thank you for it.

> Take clichés to the thrift store. They're worth less than you think. Try to come up with fresher ways to say the same stale thing a cliché would say.

> Replace your passive voice with an active voice.

> Let your manuscript rest for a day or two before you start editing.

> You'll find more errors if you print out your manuscript instead of trying to edit it on a computer screen.

> Don't let Aunt Bessie who was a 4th grade English teacher in 1975 do your editing, or your best friend who is an English major. You'll be sorry on both counts.

> Once you're done tinkering with your words, let a professional editor work his/her magic on your manuscript. Besides a graphic designer, this will be the best expenditure you'll ever make. Decide ahead of time what type of editor you want because prices vary greatly: proofreader(from .01 - .02 per word), copyeditor AND developmental editor (typically .6 - .10 cents per word with a double edit typically at .12 cents per word).

Are you in pain with all this editing "stuff?" Are you sore from moving around sentences, phrases, punctuation, storyline, and chapters? Have you replaced worn-out clichés and jargon with fresh, energetic words? If it's all just too painful to deal with, simply hire a copyeditor/developmental editor to do the heavy lifting. They're worth their weight in gold (uh oh, there goes a cliché) but so worth it as they work their magic over your manuscript.

We move on now to placing the right accents in your book as well as peeking over the ledge to see what pitfalls might be hiding in your path. Keep scrolling…we're almost ready for a housewarming party…but not quite yet. There's a little more work to do.

10

TIPPING LADDERS MAKE EVERYTHING A MESS AND ACCENT PIECES REALLY SHAPE UP A ROOM

"I love deadlines. I like the whooshing sound they make as they fly by."

— Douglas Adams

Let's cover tipping ladders first so we can get that out of the way. Research indicates that there are four main causes of ladder injuries:

1. Selecting the wrong type of ladder.

2. Using worn or damaged ladders.

3. Incorrect use of ladders.

4. Incorrect placement of ladders.

The analogy here is crystal clear. When looking out for tipping ladders in your book journey, avoid these four major pitfalls:

1. Securing "cheap" vendors. We admit, sometimes you can find a diamond in the rough on sites like Fiverr.

com, and if you stay with US-native citizens, you might have a good chance on Guru.com of finding a decent vendor for the post-writing aspects of your book. Don't set yourself up for a fall by choosing vendors solely based on pricing.

2. Procrastinating. It will only hurt you in the long run. Your book is not going to write itself.

3. Expecting perfection. Perfection is an illusion. Even though we shoot for perfection, or as close to it as possible, nobody and nothing is perfect. Even bestselling authors with dozens of books to their credit have a small amount of typos in their books; about 5% is the norm.

4. Writing and editing at the same time. We often hear, "Write with your heart, edit with your mind." The adage remains because it's true! Don't let the tipping ladder of doing both at the same time cause you to stumble within your manuscript. Write your heart out. Pour out everything you have; feel your emotions as you write, and don't worry if your nouns and verbs agree. Don't fret over sentence fragments or incomplete phrases. Just write.

Accent Pieces Really Shape Up a Room

So now that we've covered the pitfalls, it's time to add just the right accent pieces which really make a room come alive. A vase here, a flower arrangement there. Meticulously placed artwork and family photos all serve to make a room warm and inviting. Your book will need strategic accent pieces so it shines as a masterpiece.

Add the accent of a great book formatter. The authors have seen books that are so poorly formatted and put together, it's embarrassing; chapters starting on the left, blank pages where they shouldn't be, and so poorly written it's painful to turn the pages. This ought not to be! Your book represents YOUR brand and it should shine as the powerhouse brand you are!

Add the accent of a top-shelf book cover designer. Your book cover/back cover is the MOST IMPORTANT ASPECT of the entire process. A book can have mediocre content but if it has a stunning cover, it will sell. If the content is EXCEL-LENT and the cover is mediocre, it won't sell. Go figure but it's true.

Add the accent of a small- to mid-sized publisher. We recommend that you stay away from major publishing houses because you'll need to find a reputable agent to shop your man-uscript and most don't make it into the hands of a major pub-lishing house anyway...unless you're J.K.

Rowling or John Grisham. Note: a reputable agent will never ask for any money upfront. They get their fee once a publisher brings you on and pays an advance. Another note: when you get an advance AGAINST ROYALTIES that means you'll have to sell enough books to pay for that advance the publisher gave you or they could ask for all of it or a portion of it back. You'll also need to pay someone to write a marketable book proposal ($4-10k) with no guarantees it will be accepted by a major publisher. Plus, big name publishing houses will do minimal marketing for your book, they will keep most of the profits, AND take all creative control. However, with all that said, and if you're hung up on having the imprint of a Big 5 publisher stamped on the back of your book, the Authors have a teammate who can do that for you.

We believe that going with a small reputable POD(Print on Demand) publisher is one of the best ways to go. A small publisher can keep you away from the self-publishing stigma that still lies out there for some skeptics, plus a lot of the larger bookstores still shy away from self-published books because what they see is often horrifying in the way of writing, formatting, and cover design. A POD publisher is basically a pay-to-publish platform so you keep all your rights and profits. We also recommend staying far away from the factory-type, vanity publishing groups.

Another great way to go these days is self-publishing. In days gone by, self-publishing had a stigma associated with it but not anymore. With so many free tools available you can self-publish for next to nothing. What you DO want to be careful of though is not to equate self-publishing with putting out an inferior product. I've seen some horrific examples of book formatting and cover art, and believe me, you will still want to pay professionals who know what they're doing to help you produce a top-shelf product. Please don't cut corners! It's not worth your reputation, your brand, and your legacy. In this chapter you've learned about tipping ladders and how detrimental they can be to your writing journey. You've also discovered how the right accent pieces can really spruce up your writing room. All these elements fit together to bring you closer to a published book. We're almost there! We want to cover one more point in case it all seems too overwhelming.

You might find the final chapter the most beneficial of all!

11

KNOW WHEN TO OUTSOURCE

*"I am irritated by my own writing. I am like a
violinist whose ear is true, but whose fingers refuse to
reproduce precisely the sound he hears within."*

— Gustave Flaubert

Okay, so you've placed furniture in your house but it looks like someone threw the couch in with a forklift and the chairs and tables with a snow shovel. The room doesn't flow right and you know it. The paintings don't match any of the furniture or rugs in the room and the knick-knacks are misplaced. You look around, sigh, and realize you need help—the outside help of a decorator who can arrange your rooms according to proper neuroarchitecture and color palettes.

After reading this book you might be feeling the same way. You see how it can be done but you lack the writing acumen, the time, or the organizational skills to make it happen. You might start your book project, then one thing after another happens and it stalls. You mean to get back to it but it just never happens.

We have a solution for you! Outsource!!

You don't have to make it happen all on your own.

We have developed a turnkey system for getting your book written and published with minimal time and effort on your part. Of course, if you prefer a more collaborative engagement, you are welcome to actively participate in the entire process. If you choose to work with our team at Winning Proof, we'll take you through our proven process of getting that idea in your head all the way to a published book you can be proud to show off and sell back of room, on your favorite online bookseller and other book-selling outlets. The book writing process typically takes anywhere from five to twelve months depending on the complexity of your subject matter and the number of pages.

We tell would-be authors, "Tell your story and then stop." Don't get hung up on having a certain amount of pages because if you can tell your story and communicate your success principles or leadership qualities in 150 pages or less, yet you're hung up on having a 200-page book, the rest is going to be fluff and you'll lose your readers and the ultimate impact of your message.

You have almost finished your journey but there's one more important detail we need to cover…and it might be the very thing you need before your book release party. We're going to hang visual and mental artwork to keep you motivated during the entire process. Whether you plan on writing your book yourself, or outsourcing the project, you'll need daily motivational reminders to keep you going.

Read on in Chapter 12 to find out what artwork you need to hang on your writing walls. You can thank us later for equipping you with these valuable tools.

12

HOW TO STAY MOTIVATED
THROUGH THE PROCESS

"You don't write because you want to say something.
You write because you have something to say."

— F. Scott Fitzgerald

During any endeavor of significance, whether it be a new business, perfecting a new hobby, or a creative adventure like writing your book, it takes the right motivation to keep you going until the end.

Keeping yourself motivated is like hanging beautiful artwork on the walls of your new home. You need to surround yourself with reminders that this is your castle, your palace, your writing kingdom.

Behind Door #...? When you're creating your book, you will need to first identify where you stand in the motivation scale. Behind the three doors below, you will undoubtedly see yourself in at least one of them.

Behind Door #1: Here stands someone who talks about writing a book someday but never actually starts.

Behind Door #2: You see a person start their book project, all excited about it, yet they fizzle out somewhere before the finish line.

Behind Door #3: This champion starts their book project, fully commits to the end result, and in spite of any obstacles or challenges along the way, they cross the finish line; chest out, head up—the victor!

If you're like most, you're a combination of Door #1 and Door #2. You have good intentions, you think you have what it takes to make it all the way, but too many other "to-do's" get in the way. You fall to the ground when halfway through writing your book you are hit between the eyes with a massive blow of self-doubt and insecurity about your writing ability. It tackles you head-on and leaves you icing your bruised ego, and your half-finished manuscript is sidelined for good.

If you're a champion, YOU are behind Door #3!

But even the person behind Door #3 needs a boost sometimes—a shot in the arm so to speak—to get through the finish line.

That boost is often in the form of motivation—the right motivation in the right form at the right time.

Here are a few of our best strategies for staying motivated:

- To gain clarity on your message, take your book idea and put it in a seven-word sentence. This will serve as your compass so when you need motivation you can refer back to your sentence and regain focus. Think and clarify what problem or pain point you solve with your book's content.

- When you feel stuck, don't freeze, instead, ask yourself, "What's the next logical step?" Knowing where to go next is often the best motivator for continuing.

- Time yourself. Yes, actually set your timer to no more than one hour and only write for that set amount of time. No social media. No kitchen trips. Just write. If you have ADD or ADHD, set the timer for a shorter amount of time, like 20 or 30 minutes.

- Nothing like a deadline to fuel your writing! Set a reasonable deadline but just outside your comfort zone. Better yet, have your accountability partner or coach set a deadline for you – sometimes that outside pressure is just what we need to stay motivated.

- Shoot for a shorter book and you'll stay motivated to finish. As a new author, it would be a truly daunting task to try to tackle a 250-page how-to, leadership or success principle book right out of the gate. Besides, people's attention spans nowadays are short and most don't have the patience to plow through hundreds of pages. Shoot for 100-120 or so pages.

- Reward thyself! Ok, so you've set your daily word count and you've achieved that goal for a week now. As the classic commercial says, "You deserve a break today." Walk away from your computer, laptop, tablet, or lined paper, and focus on another activity. Try not to think about your writing…not even once. If an extraordinary idea hits you, log in your phone's note section and come back to it when you're ready to write again. Go to your favorite restaurant and feast. Buy your favorite ice-cream. Go to a movie you've been wanting to see. Something!

  - Post visual reminders around you.

  - Quotes that speak to your soul.

  - Mental strength quotes that toughen your resolve.

- Writing quotes like the ones in this eBook.

- Cut and tape images of a book on your monitor and/ or your bathroom mirror.

- Use anything that reminds you of your endeavor and motivates you to keep going.

Can you believe it? You've finished your journey with this book. By now you should have a really good understanding of what it takes to write and publish a book. But, really, it's only just the beginning.

Let's wrap it up.

CONCLUSION

Congratulations! You've finished your journey From Pen to Published.

We've provided you with the tools it takes to build your book from the ground up. You've learned how to effectively mindmap so you can define your ideal reader and who you would like to impact with your book. You essentially designed a floorplan for the structure of your book.

You've learned how to find the right accountability partner to keep you on track and to help you conquer any obstacles that might get in your way. You also learned how to develop a structurally sound outline to develop the framework for your book.

We looked at how to carve out specific blocks of time and we showed you some ways to focus your concentration during those blocks of time. We laid out how to create quality, organized audio recordings that allow fresh, energetic stories in and blow stale, boring stories out the window.

You discovered how to wire your manuscript by conducting thorough research to uncover facts and statistics that support your book's main theme, correctly sourcing the facts you do find, and putting spark into your manuscript by unearthing stories within the stories. We then moved to plumbing your book with three pipes: 1) your personality pipe,

2) your personal style and flair pipe, and 3) your unique mannerisms and sensory details pipe.

After the main structure is in place, you learned how to be vulnerable by showing your rough manuscript to a couple of trusted friends and colleagues for feedback. We talked about how to go about choosing the right reviewers with pure, positive motives. Then, you came to the most painful part of the journey: the editing process. You learned that it's necessary to move out what doesn't move your manuscript along, and to add just the right touches around until they fit nicely together.

You discovered that it takes more than just writing a book and leaving it on a shelf to gather dust. You now know that there are necessary post-writing pieces that will propel your manuscript from "I have an idea for a book" to "I am a published author." We discussed the importance of a good book formatter, cover designer, promo website designer, and the right publisher. We also discussed how to prevent tipping ladders, the pitfalls and dangers that can demolish your writing house.

And, in case all your newfound knowledge is just too much to take in, we've provided an outlet, a writing rescue, that requires less involvement for you yet yields the same results—a published book. Lastly, in the Bonus Chapter, you gained valuable tips on how to stay motivated throughout the entire process.

We're not going to host a housewarming party just yet. There are two more surprises for you that we think you'll really like. We've provided you with two bonus rooms to complete your book house.

Bonus rooms normally have giant screen TV's, pool tables, mini-bars or even a kitchenette, wraparound couches and overstuffed chairs, ping pong tables, maybe a book shelf, a bathroom, and definitely an abundance of snacks. Our bonus room PDF's aren't quite that elaborate but they will supply you with some potent material to add to your writing house.

But Wait...there's more!

BONUS ROOM #1:
HOW TO CRAFT A BOOK TITLE THAT SELLS

An author can name his book a certain name and it won't sell. He can make a small tweak in the title and it will become a bestseller. Go figure. No matter how you slice it, your book title is the most important marketing decision you'll ever make!

That being said, your book title is EVERYTHING, and in this case LESS is definitely more! Some of the bestsellers of all time have one, two, or three word titles. Eg: Drive by Daniel Pink, or Legacy by James Kerr, or even Talk Like TED by Carmine Gallo.

If you choose a one-word title make sure it's a potent word that, joined with your cover design and some internal depth within the pages of your book, create a one-two sales punch.

This isn't a hard and fast rule but most often the subtitle is where the how-to or the why of your book is explained, but still in just a few words.

Let's be clear here—a good title will not guarantee a bestseller. Creating a bestseller involves sales, targeted strategy, and sheer numbers, but that's another book.

Here are several bonus room tips on how to craft a book title that sells.

1. A good title should do four things:

   a. Grab people's attention

   b. Be Memorable (when people recommend your book, you want them to remember the title and not have to go searching around for keywords)

   c. Easy to say (don't make people feel stupid because they can't pronounce the name of your book)

   d. Okay for someone to say the title aloud to their friends without a flush of embarrassment coming over their face

2. A good title will be easily searchable in the Kindle kingdom (but thou shall not manipulate keywords that have nothing to do with your book just to satisfy Kindledom).

3. If your book tells the reader blatantly "How to," then say it in the title. E.g. How to Become a Circus Clown, or How to Dress a Zebra for Success.

4. Here are two title generators to get you started:

   1. https://www.portent.com/tools/title-maker

   2. http://www.adazing.com/book-title-generator/ - freet

5. Use catchy words. Former NFL player, Al Smith, created a succinct, catchy title for his book that tells you exactly what the book is about: Think Like a Pro. Act Like a Pro.

Again, the following link is just to spur your imagination:

https://www.myquickidea.com/catchy-words-list-powerful-title/

6. Tap into the experts:

   1. https://michaelhyatt.com/four-strategies-for-creating-titles-that-jump-off-the-page.html

2. https://www.thebookdesigner.com/2015/11/
    derek-doepker/

7. Test your title. Run a contest on Facebook or LinkedIn. Ask for input and take all the feedback into consideration

BONUS ROOM #2:
TOP 10 BOOK MARKETING STRATEGIES

O kay, so you've built Bonus Room #1. You've placed some great book title possibilities around the room and you're testing the position of each title to see how it fits into the overall scheme.

Now it's time for Bonus Room #2!

But before we hit Bonus Room #2, it's important to note here that going with a Big 5 publishing house does not mean they'll do a bunch of marketing for you. You'll be lucky if they actually produce a press release for you. The "big boys" of publishing save their promo dollars for authors like Stephen King and John Grisham and marques names.

Yeah, it's like that! In fact, in addition to paying a literary agent a hefty sum to write a book proposal and then shop your manuscript, the publisher will take most of the rest of what you earn on your book sales unless you're one of the super fortunate ones who hit the NYT Bestseller list in the first 24 hours by selling 9,000 books. Or, the Business Journal bestseller list by selling 3,000 in the first 24 hours. Or, you have an extra $100k - 200k laying around to throw at "buying" bestseller status.

So, you're holding a copy of your "baby" in your hands. A beautiful, bouncing semi-gloss-covered book that is your brainchild. It's the most gorgeous thing you've ever seen. YOU did this (even if you had some help)! You're so proud you could bust and you carry one with you everywhere you go so you can show off your newborn book.

Now what?

Book sales just don't happen on their own. It takes a concerted effort by you to make sure you've covered all the bases to get your book out into the world where it's supposed to go into readers' waiting hands.

Let's build Bonus Room #2 by listing the top 10 book marketing strategies:

1. Approach your local newspaper(s) where you live now and where you grew up; print media personnel love to publish "Where Are They Now?" features. Also, mine your local libraries, book clubs, and civic groups for book signings, readings, and to generally make yourself known.

2. Use very cost-effective (okay, cheap) sites like GotPrint. com to design business cards just for your book. Keep a healthy supply on hand at all times and even stuff them inside your books. OR you can get fancy and create a digital business card with a lead generation system behind it. You can also print your books using 48hrbooks.com. Winning Proof uses NextDayFlyers. com for all their business cards and other printed material. They are straight outta Compton and do really excellent, fast work.

3. Build camaraderie with your readers. Your book will include your contact email and website so log into your

email frequently to keep in touch with comments from your fans. Answer emails politely, even when a reader might not agree with everything you said in your book. Collect these emails into a contact list to announce your next book, book signing, and other promo events.

4. Bidinotto.com states that "Promotional copy is supposed to be only a teaser—not an exhaustive presentation of the story. Its job is to build curiosity, not to satisfy it. You build intense curiosity not by revealing everything, but by what you don't reveal."

5. Learn how to effectively sell your books back-of-room after a keynote speech or presentation. Again, what you're looking for is to whet a potential buyer's appetite, not stuff them full. If your speech was positive and dynamic, the audience will race over each other to buy your book at the back table. You don't have to give an "in your face" pitch if you've done your job as a speaker.

6. Decide your target market readers (not the whole world – too broad) and actively engage them yourself where they hang out. Meet your community where it lives and reads. Go to them!

WINNING PROOF OFFERS 3 EXCITING LEGACY PLAYBOOKS:

*Playbook Pricing subject to change based on market trends

1. The **Do-It-All-For-You Legacy Playbook.** You give us the idea, we'll power-talk about the main theme and general strategy, and then the Winning Proof Team will get to work. Winning Proof will provide a Legacy Builder Elite Consulting Playbook, so you know the investment required, and exactly what's included.

2. The **Consult-With-You Legacy Playbook.** You write your own book, but we'll "virtually" be right there beside you, coaching, consulting, and caring about your project the whole way through.

Per hour consulting: $150. per hour

3. The **Interviews-Only Legacy Playbook.** Don't have the current budget to write and publish your book? No problem! A Winning Proof teammate with lead you through a series of recorded, guided interviews so, at minimum, you get your story and information down on "digital" paper.

Please use the link below to schedule your 30-minute complementary call:

https://calendly.com/winningproof/30min

FAQ:

What if I need an autobiography or memoir?

Winning Proof has teammates who can get the ghostwriting done and we'll handle all the rest.

What if I want to write and publish children's books?

Absolutely! Winning Proof has children's book writers, illustrators, and editors on the team.

Do you have access to traditional publishing deals and agents?

Yes, Winning Proof has a teammate who has longstanding relationships with traditional publishers and agents. Keep in mind that most traditional publishers will want you to have a very robust mailing list and they take all creative control over your book.

What if I want to keep the lion's share of my profits and self-publish?

Winning Proof has teammates who can help you self-publish and publish via POD (print-on-demand).

Can I just produce an eBook and not a paperback?

Without a doubt, yes!

What is Winning Proof's primary genre?

Winning Proof specializes in principles-based, informational books as well as motivational, personal development, and faith-based books.

What are Winning Proof's core values?

Courage, passion, perseverance, and caring.

How long can I expect the process to take from start to finish?

That is a complex question with many variables. The answer depends on the anticipated length of your book, the complexity of the subject matter and whether research is required, and Winning Proof's project schedule. But the general answer would be anywhere from 4-5 months to a year or more.

The information in this eBook is super helpful but I want Winning Proof to write and publish my book! Tell me again…how do I start?

Please use the link below to schedule your 30-minute complementary call:

https://calendly.com/winningproof/30min

ABOUT THE AUTHORS

Brandon Williams

Brandon Williams is a former NFL Wide-Receiver, and current broadcaster, public and corporate speaker, philanthropist, business owner, and author. He's on the front lines when it comes to educating and motivating pro athletes to create enduring financial freedom. Through his pain and up's and down's from a career-ending injury, Brandon learned how to succeed and thrive despite the interceptions that life often deals unexpectedly. His passion is sharing the principles that have helped him build a successful post-NFL career life.

Equipped with entrepreneurial instincts and clarity of vision, Brandon has developed a motivational speech entitled, "How to Become an ITT Player" based on his experience with extraordinarily successful people in sports and business. He talks about what it takes to succeed at a high level. The curriculum is based on the core concepts of Persistence, Patience, Productivity and Prayer, which served as his blueprint for success. He delivers his powerful lecture about gaining strength and perseverance to overcome obstacles and life challenges to both high school and college audiences.

Distinctive excellence defines all Brandon sets out to do. Excelling as a high school athlete, he earned a scholarship to the University of Wisconsin in 2002 where he was a consistent star performer. He ended his college career in the top ten in all-purpose yards gained and was one of two people in NCAA history with 2,000 yards receiving and over 2,000 yards in returns. In the NFL, he played for the Pittsburgh Steelers, San Francisco 49ers, and St. Louis Rams. Directly after his sports career ended, he became a sports analyst for the Big Ten network and the St. Louis Rams where he currently serves as mentor and President of the St. Louis NFLPA.

The Brandon Williams Economic Development Center (BWEDC), along with St. Louis University Entrepreneurship Center, hosted the first annual Venture Draft Conference in St. Louis in 2012 where professional athletes, venture capitalists, and technology experts gathered to explore innovative business opportunities.

The conference served to provide business education and resources for athletes, and to leverage the skills learned during their athletic career into successful, post-sports professions in Information Technology. Workshops and networking sessions lead by venture capitalists and business executives were instrumental in helping attendees make informed decisions on how to capitalize on IT-related opportunities on a global level.

Brandon's education includes the University of Wisconsin's Marketing Program, completing Coldwell Banker

Gundaker Real Estate School and The NFL Broadcast Boot Camp. Additionally, Brandon hosts a national podcast called the Gridiron GQ for huddlepass.com and is an emerging author. His book, Millionaire Mindset – 7 Principles Athletes Need for Financial Freedom, is enhanced with essential principles to give aspiring professional athletes, and current professional athletes, the tools to create a blueprint for financial freedom. Brandon's success formula? Passion + Purpose = Success

Brandon is happily married to the lovely b. Marcell and they have four talented children: Jaydn, Peter, Brielle, and Blake. They currently reside in St. Louis, Missouri.

MICHELLE HILL,
YOUR LEGACY BUILDER

Michelle Hill, Your Legacy Builder at Winning Proof is a ghostwriter, book collaborator, and author of *Bathroom Prayers – Inspiring Thoughts While You're on the Pot* under the pen name, Anita Flushing. She has been writing professionally in various capacities for 25 years and specializes in helping sports and business professionals, and faith-infused individuals & companies write & publish championship-level books to build their legacies and elevate their life and career. Her vision is to change the world through the power of words.

She helps her clients break through writing blocks so they can maximize their branding playbook, increase revenue

& market share with game-winning ghostwriting and collaboration solutions. Michelle has a consistent reputation for project integrity, managing the time clock from start to finish, and making her clients feel valued.

Her game plan includes helping her clients achieve a greater level of success by writing their non-fiction books and workbooks. Michelle can take an idea or concept and move it up the field to a published book. She has recently expanded her business to include pastors, faith-based organizations, and business success & executive coaches.

Michelle has interviewed multiple high-profile sports professionals including Dan Reeves, Dick Butkus, Lee Roy Jordan, John Niland, Mike Haynes, Mike Golic, Dr. Benet Omalu, and Tony Dorsett.

Michelle is a member and/or an active part of the following organizations:

National Alliance of African-American Athletes (NAAAA)

Every.Black International Entrepreneur Mastermind Call

Regional Connections Officer at We Are Connect-ED

Triangle Entrepreneurial Leadership

Freelancers Union

Michelle has two grown kids and five grandkids, all of whom currently live in Southern California. For leisure, Michelle likes to walk, weight train, read, cook, write, and watch movies based on true events. She binge-watches The Office to unwind and laugh.

ACKNOWLEDGEMENTS

Nobody accomplishes anything alone. There's always a team effort that ignites action and passion for an endeavor. With that in mind, we'd like to thank the following people for the role they played in building this book. The Winning Proof team has an all-star roster, filled with uber-talented professionals, committed to excellence as they continue to produce top-shelf book products.

Michael Scott, MASgraphicarts.com, cover design. Michael, you never cease to amaze me with your acute design talent and eye for just the right colors and angles.

Scott Kinkade, Proofread Excelsior, you are my new best friend because you save me from many embarrassing typos. You are truly a proofreader extraordinaire. Thank you for your diligent and watchful eye that makes me look brilliant.

Amit Dey, Print Book Formatter, You are fast, diligent, and I'm super thankful for your expertise. You're on it!

BOOK THE AUTHORS TO:

- Speak at Your Next Event
- Interview on your radio or TV Show
- Be a guest on your webinar or podcast
- Conduct a Championship Book-Writing Workshop for Your Team or Organization

CONTACT INFO:

Website: winningproof.com
Email: winningproof@gmail.com
Phone: (714) 797-3731

If you have received value from this book please tell others…

- Write about From Pen to Published on your blog and social media channels.
- Suggest this book to your friends, family, neighbors, and coworkers.
- Write a positive review on your favorite online bookseller.
- Purchase additional copies for your business or sports team, or to give away as gifts.
- Feature Brandon Williams and/or Michelle Hill on your radio or television broadcast.

NOTES

www.ingramcontent.com/pod-product-compliance
Lightning Source LLC
Chambersburg PA
CBHW071418040426
42445CB00012BA/1197